Sensual divinity

A poetry collection by Ella d'Avoine

Sensual Divinity

More by Ella

The Midnight Blood Tales

Midnight Blood

The Crimson Warrior

Sensual Shadows: a poetry collection

If,

even for a fleeting moment,

a tiny voice in your mind whispers

I deserve better

listen to it.

Otherwise you will spend forever

trying to find it again.

For all the times I have been told

stop dreaming

be realistic

get your head out of the clouds

I am glad to say I never cowered.

Pity those who do not have

an entirely different world

living within their minds.

Pity those who know nothing but

the same old days around them.

For I am sure,

if I'd let go of my inner world,

my life would not be half as colourful.

I want to be a woman.

I want to be a walking piece of art

because art is not perfect.

I want to be the soul of the storm

and the heart of the moon.

I want to be kissed by the rays of the sun

and the earth beneath my feet.

I want to be full of passion and fire

and softness and strength.

I want to feel my emotions,

let them seep through the cracks in my skin

until I understand them.

I am a woman.

Before you say

that you are not capable,

turn around,

and see how far you've

already come.

She whispers to the moon.
It was the only thing that listened.
And when the daylight wakes
she misses her sister.
So she decided
I'll wear your stone around my neck
to keep our fingertips tied together.
So that even when the light beams,
I know I won't ever lose you.

-moonchild

I feel the pain
of the women who came before me.
Their agony is painted red
between my thighs.
Their suffering lines the
tension I hold in my shoulders.
Their unspoken words lie like
a stone on my tongue
that I cannot swallow.
One I will not swallow.
I've endured the pain they have
and I will not forget it.
But I am not voiceless
as they once were.
And I am sure,
that even if you were to take
my tongue from my mouth,
you would still hear me.
You would still hear *them*.

-you will not silence us forever

I could really use the sound

of ocean waves

or the delicate breeze

from the open sky.

A gentle reminder that

there are bigger things out there

than what I am feeling right now.

-open earth

You can't go through life

believing that you are broken.

Believing that you are

something that needs to be constantly fixed.

You are allowed to simply be.

Sometimes,

the most healing thing you can do

is to just be a human.

Soften

soften

soften.

You are safe.

You ran your fingers through my

hair,

and spring flowers blossomed along

my roots.

Your lips kissed mine,

and the blush of the sunset tainted

them forevermore.

You traced your fingertip down the

side of my neck,

and stars glowed and winked

beneath my skin.

You listened to me,

and the noise of waves and birdsong

sounded calmer than it had before.

-love

It's not about

strengthening your intuition,

it's about

strengthening your trust

in your intuition.

I could write an entire story

on the girl I used to be.

It amazes me,

how strong she was.

How she got up every morning

despite the way people spat at her,

despite the way they laughed when

she turned her back.

It amazes me,

that despite all of it,

her smile was still so full of kindness.

It amazes me,

that she'd willingly give her love,

folded neatly with a handwritten note,

to those who did not cherish it

the way it deserved to be.

I strive to be her every single day.

I am proud to hold her qualities.

And I am proud

to have never gotten rid of them

despite the cruelty of the world.

Despite the many times
I wanted to wish away my softness
for something made of stone.

There is always tomorrow.

I am equal.

Equal parts light-hearted,

gentle touches and lips

as I am powerful,

rough hands and burning desire.

I will strive to embrace both.

To let them speak together,

rather than separately.

When my soul is tired,

cracked and bleeding,

I seek the comfort of the night.

The quiet, dead hours

of its blackness

so I have to think of nothing at all.

But,

when my soul glows

and cheeks ache with joy,

I crawl into bed with a smile along my lips

and whisper goodnight to the darkness.

Thank you for cradling me.

-the night is not something to fear

You are not here

to be understood.

You are here

to understand yourself.

Be the woman
your inner child always dreamed
of being.

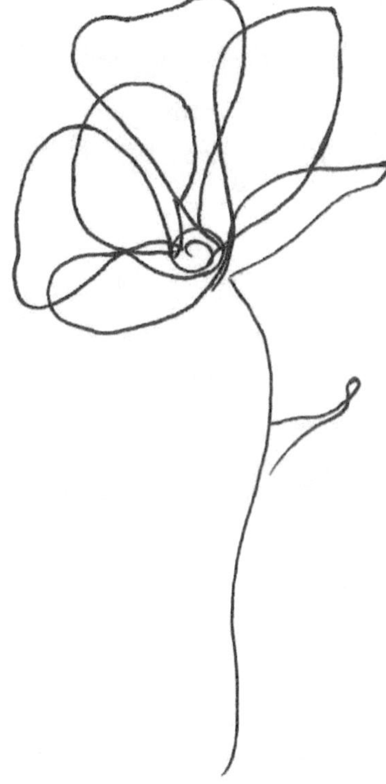

I found my femininity

in the curve of my bare hip,

the kindness of my smile,

the light of my eyes,

the red of my lips,

the softness of my breast.

Femininity found me through strength.

Through bravery.

Through authenticity.

I once never knew the softness of it.

The wholeness of divinity.

Now, it does not matter where I find it,

for I know that it has always been within me.

-sensual divinity

It had been quiet all day.

Perhaps even sunny.

Lost to my mind,

I didn't register how the light died

and the room darkened.

Then the rain came,

heavy and loud,

and it reminded me that

even the sky needs to cry sometimes.

I do not strive to be perfect.

I merely strive to be the sexiest,

kindest,

softest version of myself.

-a promise

Carved from the budding flower

and painted with its pollen and grace,

her breath is like a whisper of the wind,

gently tangling its soothing fingers

into your hair.

Sewn with the moon's rock

and star's fire in her skin,

she glows and glitters

forevermore through the blackness.

She feels deeply,

cares with her beating heart

stuffed in her sleeve.

And she now appreciates who she is,

for she is no longer wishing it away for

something made of stone.

-gentle soul

Glitter dappled skin

always shining through dark.

Though the moon was always what she looked

for

in moments where she couldn't tell

if her eyes were open or closed.

And even when her pain consumed her,

she remained pure and white,

for she knows both dark and light.

-balance

The more my femininity swells,

the more life around me glows.

Oh, how blind I'd been

to stifle that golden force within me.

The eternal emit of glitter.

My femininity is dear to me.

I dare not speak against her greatness.

But I will always remember the girl

who fought so hard

against the woman she was trying

to become.

I remember a time

where the bareness of my chest would make

me uncomfortable.

I have come so far from then.

In moments where I don't feel connected,

it is easy to remind myself

of the love I hold for me.

I sit with my bareness,

my skin vulnerable and raw,

for there is no simpler way to learn to love me.

-naked

My dear girl,

do not let this world make you believe

that love is hard,

impossible,

or unreachable.

Love is in the birds when they

sing in the morning.

Love is in the little smile you

give yourself in the mirror.

Love is reachable

and absolutely attainable.

Do not let this world harden you.

Do not let this world stop you

from dreaming.

Do not let this world stop you

from *believing*.

Like the clouds, you will cry.

Like the sky, you will darken.

Like the storms, you will strike.

But do not forget that also,

like the sun, you will shine.

-dark days don't last forever

I have walked many a patch of soil.

The flesh of my feet remembers

the drop and dip of the earth.

But it does not tame the unease in my being.

It is a restless begging.

A writing pleading.

Salvation

it calls.

I do not know how to calm it.

I'm not used to living without chaos.

It is weaved

within the hard skin of my feet,

damned to be there until I untangle it.

Even in the biting dark of the winter,

when my toes meet the sleeping earth,

I feel the pulse beneath it.

The thrum of the heart I stand on.

The plants lean for my touch,

for they too

recognise the howling call of chaos in my skin.

And though

I yearn to run with the wolves,

and sleep with bay leaves beneath my tongue,

I dare not open the bottle of chaos

in this world.

For it would not accept me.

So in the darkness of the night,

when the pleading writhes and begs,

perhaps once again,

I say to it,

but in another life.

-a witch in another life

You don't have to stay loyal
to your pain.
If life starts to get better again,
allow it.
Pain is not a badge of honour
that you must hold onto.
You deserve some happiness.

She found love
tucked into the pages of
her favourite book.
She found love
in the gentle scent of
her favourite perfume.
She found love
in the feel of silk against
her soft, morning skin.
She found love
in the last rays of
the dying sun.
She found love
in all she did.

There is something intrinsically beautiful

about the storm before the sun.

Chaotic and turbulent.

Frantic and heavy.

I sat with the storm last night,

let it wreak its havoc,

there was no use in trying to stop it.

And what I found was a blessing.

Pain shows where peace is not yet.

Medicine is found within that pain.

So today,

I am kissing the storm goodbye,

gently on the cheek,

because without it

I never would've found the sun.

Dwell in pleasure.

I remember the day it came back to me.

I woke up feeling odd that morning,

for my power had not been something

I'd felt in a long time.

It was like a glittering wind,

sweeping softly over my naked skin

as it painted me.

I remember going for a walk that morning,

it was early,

there was no one on the beach with me.

I dipped my fingers into the ocean,

one with the great water,

and I remember wondering where had it been

all this time?

Where had I been?

But when the chill of the sea

swept up my hand,

that thought fell away,

replaced with one far more important

that would smother all doubt

for the rest of my days.

-the morning I found myself again

May life kiss your cheeks
and leave you blushing.
May life be the lover
you have been waiting for.

There's a kind of magic

in being a girl.

Magic that I've found

if you do not hold onto tightly,

can be taken from you.

To every girl that did lose her magic,

therefore growing into a woman

who wasn't sure who she wanted to be,

or who she was,

connect with that girl again.

The girl who knew her magic

even with her eyes covered.

The girl whose magic glittered,

dusting and dappling every soul she met.

Find her.

Because she will show you the way.

There is something

wholly intimate

about waking early before

the rest of the world,

and sitting with yourself and the earth

just as you are.

Be brave, my love.

I am not deterred

by the stretch of my skin

that paints lines across my thighs.

I am not sickened

by the softness of my belly.

I am not repulsed

by the loudness of my voice

when something excites me.

I am not disgusted

by the smaller curve of my breast.

No.

I am infatuated

with the lines across my thighs.

I am enamoured

with the softness of my belly.

I am bewitched

with the excitement in my voice.

I am enraptured

with the delicate curve of my breast.

All my life you have told me differently.

Taught me to hate my own skin.

But today I laugh,

go ahead,

my voice shakes as I tell you so,

string me up for not meeting your standards.

When I know I speak for all the women around

me.

You will never change me.

You will never change us.

-a letter to society

I dream to be the kind of woman
who always holds a gentle space for others.
To let life flow through me,
rather than struggle against it.
To embody the ripples of a river,
constantly moving,
constantly peaceful.
I dream to be the kind of woman
who puts sweetness before stress,
who knows that the divine is always
on her side.
I dream to be the kind of woman
who honours the serenity and stillness
of her being.
Who would never put that divinity
at risk.
I dream to be the kind of woman
who doesn't waste away her time,
and instead,
uses every second of it
creating something beautiful.

She is a magician,

creator of her reality.

She is a goddess,

sweetness pouring from her skin.

She is an empress,

a twin of mother earth herself.

She is a phoenix,

the ashes are her rebirth.

A flower that blooms in darkness,

is the most beautiful of them all,

for it knows the balance

of both day and night.

Love didn't break you.

Someone who didn't understand love did.

Do not be scared to love again.

It is the simplest and most beautiful thing.

Don't be afraid to be sexy.

Wear your favourite dress,

just because you can.

Dance,

just for you.

Your sensuality

deserves to be embraced.

When you're trying to find yourself,

steer away from the world's influence.

You don't have to be told what to be,

or how to be,

and you will only find yourself within.

I can hear the whispers in the

sunlight's beams.

The secrets of the morning dew

and the ever-moving energy of the trees.

The sounds of the water stir my soul,

like calling to like.

The moonlight makes me grow,

heals my tired limbs,

fuels the stars to glow.

And when I thread my fingers

through the grass,

I can feel the sturdy heart

beating like it has always done,

no matter how old.

I can hear you, feel you.
Never stop speaking to me.

-earthling

Scarlet lips

and kind smiles.

The taste of cherries

and scent of roses.

Rays of the sun

and sweetness of honey.

The freshness of rain

and twinkle of the stars.

-she is Venus embodied

You are not for everyone.

Your energy is radiant,

magnetic,

ethereal.

You are your own muse.

You make love to life

and create forever beauty.

You are sacred

and you treat yourself as much.

You take care of your softness.

You are a thing of utter

beauty and serenity,

and you allow your authenticity

to always shine through.

Never change.

You are beautiful.

-dear divine feminine

I feel like coffee in the morning,

autumn rain and twilight stars.

I feel like soft skin beneath the sheets,

delicate touches and birdsong.

I feel like warm, early mornings,

sweet roses and sunlight.

I feel like scarlet lips,

black lace and silky smiles.

I feel like fresh earth in the dead of night,

wild wolves and rose thorns.

I feel like the light of a moonstone,

the glitter of the stars and howl of the

darkness.

-the many sides of me

When there are people out there

who would pluck the stars from the sky,

just for you,

why would you settle for anything less?

I am unashamed of the love

that I pour into everything.

I don't fear looking silly,

or being perceived

as too much,

because love is an eternal source.

Feel the fear,

and do it anyway.

Within every woman there is

a healer,

a goddess,

a warrior,

a witch,

a mother.

You are absolute magic.

Glitter-soaked and rose-flavoured,
there is something magical about her,
something moon-made about her.
Dawn-blushed and star-scented,
there is something divine about her,
something sun-kissed about her.

I'm not quite sure

how to order the words that are stuck in my

throat.

I don't think they'd make much sense.

They'd be like raindrops

falling onto wilting flowers.

Beautiful and delicate perhaps,

but confusing and misunderstood.

I wanted to write.

I wanted to write something

beautiful.

But I guess this is,

because it is me.

It is me feeling.

And I would rather feel it all,

good and bad,

than feel nothing at all.

-it doesn't make sense, and that's okay

I look at birds from time to time.

Wondering whether life would feel

freer

if I were one with them.

If I were able to soar above the clouds,

dance with the wind,

sing the sweetest songs.

Until one day I remembered,

I have wings of my own.

They are merely waiting

to be used.

You are made of oceans and stars.

You are created from sugar and honey.

You are sewn with flames and rose petals.

You are hemmed with rain and moonlight.

Crafted by the universe, one might say.

So when you doubt yourself,

you are doubting a force greater than us all.

Throw yourself at the world

and see what happens.

I've come to realise that

symmetrical is boring.

Perfect is boring.

There is uniqueness to you.

A character that is

one of a kind.

You have things that no one else does.

And that will always,

always,

be more than enough.

Love me deeply,

or do not love me at all.

Embrace your deep sensitivity.

It is a gift,

to feel so deeply.

Your body can pick up on things,

that your eyes can't see.

I know that in a world like this,

it almost seems easier

to hide it all away.

To turn it off and pretend

that you don't feel as deeply as you do.

But this world needs you.

It needs your love,

your kindness,

your light.

We have lost our way and

lost sight of our true selves.

It is natural to feel everything deeply.

To feel the sunsets in your heart

and the stars in your smiles.

Don't let this world

tell you differently.

Honour your sensitivity with every breath,

and remember just how badly

this world needs *you*.

When a goddess wants something,

she creates it.

She doesn't need force,

or struggle.

She has divinity

and frequency.

She has utter faith in both herself

and the divine.

And what she creates

flows to her with beautiful ease.

Like the moon you will wane

you will grow dark and shadowed,

you may even lose your way.

But like the moon you will also beam,

casting shadows over the earth

with your mighty gleam.

-you will shine again

Hone your fierceness like a **blade,**

and nurture your softness like **silk.**

Poems for the seven female archetypes

A lifeforce energy
buzzing beneath honey coated skin,
as glittering as the golden sun rays,
her passion is like no other.
Creativity flows from her fingertips
like waterless rivers,
bountiful in their beauty.
She paints with the blush of the sun,
writes with the crescent of the moon,
sings with the wind in the sky,
and loves with sugar on her lips.
She is vast and deep,
a never-ending sea of adoration,
that she carries with her
everywhere she goes.

-the lover

They may underestimate her.

For her youth and kindness

do not show you the

strength she has within.

It is unknown to others,

how much she knows.

How deep her knowledge goes.

How much she has seen.

But my,

she is beautiful.

Like the rosy reflection of a sunrise

on glittering ocean water.

So don't look at her big, bright eyes

and see someone who knows nothing.

For she is the first budding flower

of all femininity.

-the maiden

Her words are sweet and gentle,

warm enough to chase away

winter's cold bite.

She is the rock against which

the sea crashes,

unmoving in her strength.

She stands as tall and sturdy

as a great oak.

She is the outstretched hand to all

that are suffering,

her comfort like a cool breeze

on a scorching day.

She is a leader,

supporting all generations to come.

-the mother

Across her shoulders

sits the jewels of a kingdom.

Her skin,

draped in pearls and rubies,

radiates a strength that it utterly

unforgettable.

Her voice,

carried to the very corners of the earth,

throbs with power and confidence.

She is the shining butterfly,

and her presence is not one that

you can miss.

-the queen

Lined with precision

and dipped in ferocity,

she is the ultimate archer.

A protector of the women around her.

She runs with the wolves

and dances with the lions.

Howls into the night

and laughs with the firelight.

You will see her footprints in the earth

from where she walks with the stars.

Wild and free

she will forever be.

-the huntress

Ever-changing,

she is devoted to her growth.

Waning and waxing

just as the moon.

She's a seeker of truth

and she bleeds inner knowing.

With all eyes open

there is nothing she doesn't see.

She radiates lavender,

it curls off her in glittering waves,

giving all around her the sight they

so desperately seek.

-the sage

Her inner world is luminous.

A soft bed of flowers and butterflies,

buzzing with life and peace.

She knows herself deeply,

understanding her waters to their very corners,

tracing her fingers along the seabed of her soul

until she knows its patterns with her eyes

covered.

Vines inked into her skin,

mist smoking in her eyes,

she knows all before it happens,

connected so vastly to the divine.

-the mystic

Create enough space within you

to allow all parts of you,

both light and dark,

to coexist

in harmony.

In a world that's harsh,

be kind.

Though the world has given me

many reasons to think otherwise,

I will never not believe in love.

I will always believe in the light

at the end of the tunnel.

I will always believe that actually

love is simple and beautiful

and absolutely attainable.

I will always believe that the trees

wave at us when they dance with the wind.

I will always believe that the love I dream of,

the love that little me dreamed of,

is out there somewhere.

I will always believe in love

in all its forms.

-a romantic at heart, always

You tell me to dim myself,

and I say,

would you tell a butterfly

to carve off its wings?

May you feel the wrath

of the women who came before me.

May you feel their fire and blood

burn and stain your skin

for the injustice you rained upon me.

May you never forget your wrongdoings

as they etch themselves into you,

burdened to be there forevermore.

May you feel the weight of the pain you caused

as nature howls around you,

resorting the balance

you destroyed.

-injustice

There is a small window

carved into the sloping tile of the roof.

Two arms,

crossed with her chin resting against them,

she gazes at the view.

She watches the seasons fade and bloom.

Enjoys the mist of the winter

and the green of the spring.

On some days the wind tangles her hair,

on others the sun kisses her nose.

She is always watching from that window.

Not judging nor spying.

Just gazing.

Gazing at life

with all the childlike wonder one should carry.

If you ever spot her,

eyes sparkling and hair glowing,

smile to her.

For she holds life like a soul

holds it new vessel.

With all the love and gentleness

one can muster.

85

-the attic window

I am ready

to be gentle and kind

with myself as life

greets me every morning.

It's a gift

to know oneself deeply.

To find comfort in your own heart,

to see your body as your home.

When you learn

every little quirk and kink

that your body holds,

you can be your greatest friend.

It's somewhere between
a yearning and a blessing,
this feeling.
Somewhere between
an ache and a medicine.
Somewhere between
nervous butterflies and untamed fire.
I experience everything with you,
through you,
and it makes me wonder whether you are
the entire universe itself,
balled up into one beautiful being.

Move forwards with love,

always.

Allow the love you've already given

to fill the world.

Free yourself from the past.

You do not have to look back in anger.

Every time you abandon your core beliefs,

you disconnect from yourself.

You owe it to yourself

to stay loyal and true to all

that you believe in.

It may be hard to,

in a world like this,

but once you do,

that is *freedom*.

Something was rotting inside of me.

I felt the gaping hole grow,

like a never-ending landslide,

curling in around the edges,

hiding from the stench of the pain.

But here I lie with you,

my nose in your neck,

here I blur into you,

ebb and flow with you,

and I forget that there was ever any

darkness within me.

Believe me when I tell you

that there is a day,

somewhere in your future,

where you'll look back and something will

click.

It'll be like breathing

after years underwater.

It'll be like seeing the sun

after a long winter.

And you'll think,

oh,

that is why everything happened.

And in that moment,

all the hardship you endured will feel

absolutely and irrevocably

worth it.

-trust the process

Power,

pleasure,

ease,

peace,

they are all so unknown to us.

Oh, how I wish the women of this world

never once had a reason to doubt themselves,

hide themselves,

or to believe that they were not enough.

Let our pain become a lesson,

may we all heal from it,

so our daughters do not grow up

in the same world

that we did.

You could take all the skin from my bones,

and from her bones,

and under it all you would find

that we are the same.

You could take the skin from your bones,

and despite your anger and disgust,

you'd find those same white bones

that you found in me and her.

It is no crime to accept what you know to be

true.

Beneath it all,

we are all the same.

-equality

May love find you

in everything you do.

Speak up.

Let your voice be heard.

Let your shouts rattle the stars.

Let your screams create tsunamis.

They will not silence us.

We are stronger

when we speak up.

I am convinced

that the stars could implode,

the seas could dry out,

the sun could burn itself barren,

and I would still find my way back

to you.

Because I am a woman.

I am deep

and I am sensitive.

I can be strong

but I want to be soft.

I am a warrior in spirit but that

does not make me unfeeling.

It is not my job to harden.

You may try to tear me from my softness

but you will not succeed.

Your body isn't a coffin

for all that has happened to you.

Give your pain somewhere to live

that is not within you.

Weave it into your writing,

your singing,

your dancing,

your painting.

Let it be consumed by art

and devoured by love.

-turn your pain into beauty

It will all be okay.

Create for yourself,

and yourself only.

Creativity is an outlet for pain,

a home for love,

and a bed for expression.

It is okay

if no one but you understands it.

No other needs to understand it.

Your creativity is you,

just in a different

but no less beautiful form.

"You think I'm beautiful?"

All women are.

There is a feeling that comes

right before life changes.

It's like

little sparks in the air around you,

popping and fizzing with excitement.

I have been through so much.

To finally feel peace within a body

that I have fought against for so many years,

makes all the bloody hands and teary eyes

absolutely worth it.

Go right through the pain.

Fighting it,

or attempting to go around it

does not fix the ailment.

You must go right through it.

And remember,

there is always sunshine waiting

on the other side for you.

If you ever wonder

whether you're missing out,

or you're late in life,

remember that you cannot be **behind**

in your own story.

Remember that
adversity and doubt
are always at their loudest
as they die.
And that is *always*
right before the change happens.

There has been a change within me.
My heart no longer hangs heavy
and my head is no longer
so loud.

You are worth loving.

Worth saving.

Worth healing.

You are worthy of it all.

Anyone who makes you feel otherwise

isn't for you.

I vowed to never let my pain consume me

to the point where it began

hurting others.

My pain is mine and mine alone,

which is not to say I should struggle alone,

but it should never have me

in such a chokehold that I can't

stop it from spewing its venom

at other people.

'I wanted nothing more than to sew myself into his existence, so I was with him even when I was nothing but dust.'

-Midnight Blood by Ella d'Avoine

Look at how beautiful your **soul is.**

Life has no choice

but to reflect that back to **you**

in one way or another.

Remember that beauty,

real beauty,

is far deeper, far vaster,

and far more passionate

than something as short lived as

physical appearance.

Just because you don't know
how or when
something is going to happen,
shouldn't be a reason for you to give up on it
happening at all.

Creative souls are my favourite kind of people.

They could go through the most

gut-wrenching experience,

and turn around a few months later

with a sewn-up heart,

and the most beautiful piece of art.

I have flowers on my bedside table,

a warm duvet over my legs,

the berry scent of my favourite candle

is lingering in the air,

and the sweet taste of my coffee

still dances on my tongue.

Maybe everything really is okay after all.

My favourite song is playing in the

background,

I'm writing poetry in the notebook I found

by chance one day and utterly fell in love with,

it's dark outside and I am completely

encompassed by the sheer

romance of my solitude.

Everything really did turn out okay.

Maybe tomorrow will be filled with

warm hearts and sunlight.

Maybe I don't have to dread the days ahead

before they even come to me.

Maybe,

just maybe,

after all the darkness of the past,

my heart will heal.

And I am sure that the simplicity

of this very moment,

is enough to do exactly that.

There was a girl once.

A girl who dreamed of glitter and gold,

for the world she lived in

provided neither.

All looks well for the girl who dreams.

Continually lost to her imagination kept her

busy.

Kept the darkness quiet.

I will never forget that girl.

I've been so stuck in the future,

stuck in the past,

stuck anywhere that is not right here,

right now.

There are endless possibilities for me

in this very moment.

This very moment where I am breathing,

where I am feeling whatever I am feeling.

And I am totally,

completely,

infinite.

There is something inherently human about

overlooking pain.

Forgetting it, ignoring it.

No one finds it comfortable to feel.

I've realised that I've been sat behind clouds,

clouds I created myself,

to mask the suffering.

To keep me safe.

Deception has kept me company for

a few years too many.

People have ripped the skin from my bones,

and I have let them.

They've torn it with their teeth,

shredded it,

discarded it,

until I was nothing more than bone.

All it took was one word.

One moment to let the memory

unblur and reveal itself to me once again.

I have made myself a promise now,

for I am smarter and stronger than I once was,

that I would rather

bite the skin from my own bones,

than let another lay their hands on me.

-the clouds of my own deception

Soften, soften, soften.

The feminine energy begins to radiate

when a woman allows herself to be soft and

kind

to both herself and others.

Dear girl,

please do not let them tie your wings

and stop you from soaring.

Like a flower,

unfurling its petals at dawn,

I feel the missing pieces of myself

begin to yawn.

And it is then that I realise,

they weren't missing at all,

they were simply waiting

for me to call.

May you find a love

that always holds a soft space

for your many deaths and rebirths.

And I did this.

I fucking did this.

I was brave and broken and bruised and

courageous and angry and kind and soft and I

healed and I fucking did this.

I changed my life for the better because

somewhere inside me,

even when I was utterly lost and had absolutely

no idea who I was,

I still fought for a better life because I knew

that there was one for me.

I knew that there had to be something better

because goodness does exist,

and I always looked for it.

Allow yourself to flow like water,

and that water will carry

the passionate fire that burns within you.

Who's to say that you cannot

have both untamed flames

and soft rivers

within the chasm of your soul?

I have flowers in my skin,

stars glittering in my eyes,

berries smeared over my lips,

and crimson in my hair.

Each created, birthed, and moulded,

from different parts of my life.

I am a walking memoir

of my experiences.

You could instantly spot her in a crowd of

people,

a golden, glowing needle

in a dull and grey haystack.

You couldn't mistake her hair,

flowing gently in the warm breeze,

or her skin gleaming

under the early summer sky,

or her smile,

her real smile,

the one she covers up too often.

There was her nose, her scars,

her slightly wonky eyebrows,

her lips, her hips, and everything else in

between.

But what stood out was her eyes,

like two individual skies,

vast and deep and knowing.

And when she looked at you,

she saw you,

and you wondered how you'd gone so long

without being truly seen like this.

Just because you carry everything so well

doesn't mean it isn't heavy.

You're allowed to put it down.

Remember that.

You know the old saying - if a tree falls in an

empty forest, does it actually make a sound?

Just because no one heard it,

doesn't mean it didn't happen.

Healing is a little like that.

Just because you shatter and crumble

in your empty bedroom in the

early hours of the morning,

does not mean your pain is not real,

nor does it mean it didn't truly happen.

-you don't have to prove that your pain exists

for it to be real

When people ask me why I write, more often than not, I'm not sure what to say.

How do I convey such a beautiful thing?

How do I say that the normal way of life repels me, for I find no inspiration in the tiresome circles it would bring to my eyes.

How do I convey the sheer sunlight joy it brings me to live slowly, to spend my days alone with my beautiful words.

How do I say that this is not something I could give up and leave behind me, even if I wanted to.

I live and breathe words. And yet, can't always find the right ones to explain just how much it all means to me.

-a writer's emotions

Be wild,

untamed,

full of passion,

and dripping with freedom.

My heart beats for you today and always.
For the life you hold in your veins,
the love in your chest.
For the softness you bring to a sharp world,
the richness in your smile.

The soul of a dragon.
The wings of a Phoenix.
The breath of the moon.
The heart of the earth.

A reflection of the divinity
you hold in your womb.
A ray of moonlight shimmering over your skin.
A gentle kiss to a furrowed brow.
My heart beats for every woman today.
Free or chained.
My heart beats for you all.
May you never forget your divinity.

May you hold it within you
and let it shine for all to see.
May you give yourself the softness
you deserve today.

There's something about the word *you*.

It has so much weight to it,

so much density,

so much unrequited power.

It could be spat like poison

or whispered like honey.

Spoken softly in the morning,

the sunlight glistening over your lover,

or screamed,

the word lined with anger

and the pieces of a shattered heart.

What power that one word has.

To hold or to break.

To soothe or to shatter.

To adore or to poison.

-you

It is no evil thing

to look at yourself with kindness,

awe, and pride.

This life was never meant

to be a burden.

One thought has been constant

throughout my life.

But today,

for the first time,

I really feel like I'm hearing it.

I wish someone would love me like I loved.

A plea, perhaps, rather than a thought.

A begging plea that crawled out of the

hollowness that gaped within my chest.

Forever bleeding, forever empty.

Words that are barely a mouthful,

but carry the scorn of thousands.

I want to change that today.

For I have realised that the hollowness

within me is no longer there.

What it yearned for was not what I expected,

yet greater than I could've ever imagined.

That thought, that plea, it doesn't sit right with

me anymore.

for my heart is no longer bleeding.
Today, that thought changes.

What a gift it is to feel my own love within me.
To feel what others feel
when I share my light.
What a gift, that all of that love is mine.

I find beauty in the simple things.

In the taste of my coffee,

the view of the hills from the car,

in the song of the birds in the morning,

and the feeling of the early sun on my skin.

In the sparkle of water in the summer,

the breeze that blows the clouds over the sky,

in the sweetness of the flowers in bloom,

and the tickle of the leaves across my palms.

These things remind me that I am alive,

and that everything is alive with me.

Look for a love that is

all encompassing.

Not all consuming.

Be sure.

Be sure in your own visions,

in your own creativity.

Be sure in your passions,

in who you are as a person.

Be so sure in yourself,

and in everything that you **do**,

that no other opinion

can sway you.

Like a fire,

you cannot be tamed.

You cannot be groomed or controlled

forever.

And like a flower you will grow

through the cracks of their cage,

stronger than they ever would've believed.

-it's okay to outgrow places

Her aura is peaceful.

She gives softness to life,

and life gives her love back.

Her entire essence is beautiful,

glittering gold and sweet like roses.

She fought hard to be this version of herself,

and for that,

she will always put herself first.

-you deserve love from yourself

Despite what this world tells you,

your body needs softness.

Humans are inherently gentle

and loving.

It's just that somewhere along the way,

we've lost ourselves.

Let me be the one to tell you,

that it is okay to find yourself again.

That it is okay for you to rest,

to be gentle and kind.

This world doesn't need any more

harsh truths or tough love,

it desperately needs kindness.

She is made of dreams,

and not meant for this world.

And though she doesn't know it yet,

what she thought was her downfall,

would be the one thing to change

this world forever.

Winter evenings are full of cosy warmth.

Spring mornings are full of sunlight.

Summer twilights are full of stars.

Autumn afternoons are full of a soft, chilly

bite.

May you wake on each of these days,

and feel the magic in the air around you.

May it remind you what a privilege it is

to be alive.

And when I'm in my favourite place,

the smell of stories dancing in the air,

my head is no longer so loud.

-bookshops

You are so much more

than what happened to you.

You are so much more than your pain,

than the deep feelings that hurt you.

I know it feels endless,

like the agony won't ever cease,

but the only constant is change.

Even pain is temporary.

One day you will look back and realise

that it no longer hurts as much.

And that day is absolutely worth

fighting for.

It's time to start walking

like you've got thousands of goddesses

behind you.

You're here for a divine reason, my love,

so you better hold your head fucking high.

There is undeniable peace
in wandering alone.
In spending your days immersed in
romantic solitude.
Oh, if only I had known,
that wandering aimlessly would
lead me back to myself.
I would've done it much sooner.

Magic does exist.

You just have to be willing

to find it.

I hope you know just how incredible you are,
for keeping your heart open
even after everything that this world
put you through.

The candlelight flickered in her eyes,

and she watched it dance over the walls.

The rain cried onto her windows,

its peaceful sound warming her veins.

That was the night she realised

how calm she'd become.

How much she had fought,

how much she had won.

And she knew that she'd keep battling,

until the rain no longer cried,

and the candlelight died.

You see glitter in the sunlight,
even on the dark days.
You find the warm kiss of contentment
in your coffee every morning.
You let your passions swallow you,
constantly growing and changing into
the woman you've always wanted to be.
And you have always known,
despite what the world told you,
that you've always been complete.
You, darling, are everything.

Keep writing.

Keep creating.

Never, ever, stop expressing yourself.

The world wants to see you,

and you deserve to be heard.

I did not come here to dim myself.

I did not come here to be only a fraction

of who I truly am.

I hold the pain and power

of the women who came before me,

and they stand at my sides as I vow

to make a difference.

So if you are a woman,

and you are reading this,

remember who you are

and who came before you,

because their blood runs in your veins,

and fire burns in your heart.

-about *Sensual divinity*

Even though Ella didn't know it then, *Sensual divinity* was birthed many years ago, in the form of a stunning, green journal she found in Waterstones one afternoon. For three years she wrote in it whenever life got a little too overwhelming, letting her feelings bleed all over the pages and mould into sonnets. And when she found the journal earlier this year, having forgotten about it for a very long time, she knew that it would become something even more beautiful than it already was.

I wanted to make a difference with this collection. Even though our world is changing, female voices are still underheard and underappreciated. I hope that this book has reminded you that it is absolutely okay to be your raw and real self. To be a woman is an incredible thing, and for the world to truly see this, we must first see it in ourselves.

-about the author

Ella is a fantasy author from a little forest in the UK. Her hobbies include tattoos, coffee, books, and pretty jewellery. She's a proud witch, though promises that she's not here to convert you. She's been writing ever since she could walk, and little her is super proud of how much she's achieved.

You can find Ella as @elladavoine on Instagram and TikTok for your own entertainment, or at www.edavoineauthor.com

www.ingramcontent.com/pod-product-compliance
Lightning Source LLC
Chambersburg PA
CBHW030931060726

47591CB00005B/1750